PREFACE

I have always lived in a separate world inside of myself, self-created, ethereal, apart from this earthly place. A world created with words I turned into poetry. I made more sense in my world, less abstract than I am here on earth. It was safer in the ethereal. The outside world was very scary to me as a kid, didn't make much sense to me. I was always too afraid to speak, so quiet I kept until I found the pencil and the paper. I never shared with anyone; it was mine to take with me to my tomb. Writing helped me release all that was buried, all that burdened me, all that enchanted and excited me. Writing inside my world no one could ever judge me, and that was a comfort to me. My writing journey never started as poetry. It started as short stories that told of my world inside my head.

Since I can remember, my mom the avid reader, forced me to the library with her almost every day. I didn't want to be there, so with the toys I played while she found the books that helped her escape. For years like clockwork to the library we trekked. It wasn't until I was about 7 or 8 that I picked up a book and read it. A romance novel. I liked it and so I read a few more. Then I found children's books, playful, colorful, imaginative stories. I liked some of those too. Then I found stories to tell after dark and goosebumps. I enjoyed those a lot. One day while floating down the grown-up aisles, I landed at the poetry section. The first book I touched with my fingertips was by Edgar Allen Poe. I was immediately hooked. I read it all and wanted more. Our next time at the library I found an anthology about love, heartache and tragedy. I knew nothing of these things but felt like somehow I did. As if my soul and spirit were already familiar with it. From those days forth, my short story telling slowly morphed into my own poetry writing.

My poems started very innocent, a bit naïve as a kid would be. My childhood was rough, but when I wrote I pretended it was something completely different, pretty. As I grew older, apparent teenage angst showed through. My early adult years is when I began to really experience the underbelly of multiple traumatic events. Ironically those events would cultivate and shape me into the writer I would eventually become. I was now experienced in life's trials and tribulations. I always asked why me? Then I came to see I could share how it is possible to come out on top from the deepest depths of underneath. I had no idea where it would all take me. I wanted to keep it secret. I was still afraid to speak to others even through my writings.

It was the day when the love of my life took her last breath that all of my life's traumatic experiences culminated into creating this book. It was then that I understood exactly what I felt was so familiar as a kid, the love, the tragedy, the heartache of losing the person you love and the darkness that comes with it. Due to the past traumas I experienced, I learned how to detach and barricade myself inside of myself. I was never planning on sharing any of it.

One afternoon after a work function, I met the love of my life who changed everything I thought I knew about the world. I finally felt safe, and things made sense. My soul mate, the one I gave my entire being to. I loved hard, harder than I ever intended. When she passed away, it shattered everything I knew to be true. I stopped writing, talking, working; I stopped living. I became a human ghost wandering lost, not accepting or believing what really happened.

For over 2 years, I battled my many demons that I barricaded and locked inside what I thought was an impenetrable box. After my love passed away, I wandered into every dark corner blindly; alcohol and drugs became my new best friends and my worst enemies. That is until the night I almost died from an overdose. I awoke from not just death, but the death of my old self. That day forward my goal was to get sober. I did and everything changed. I began writing again. It was the only thing I could think of to ease my agonizing pain. This is where the birthing of this book begins.

I made the decision to share with you what my world from the outside and inward looks like, sounds like, tastes like, feels like, hurts like and loves like. The secrets of my soul in this book I Bare. I have learned it is my purpose now to share. My words Have helped me heal and I hope can help heal others. We are never alone.

All My Love,

~SOJOURNA

Beautifully Broken Blue Butterfly
(#BBBB)
A collection of poetry about Love, Grief and Hope

Poetry By: SOJOURNA

CONTENTS

The Road to You…

My Juvenile

Young love
Naïve to a touch
Unsure about what to give up
The meaning of vulnerability not understood
I've walked through life with rose colored glasses on
Met mistake after mistake
Heartache after heartbreak
They were all just a prelude to you
To prepare me to live dangerously in love
Intentional
Unconditional
Into my life came you
Living your life to the fullest
Your juvenile perceptions I admired about you
You scared me
You were excitingly, intelligently reckless
My opposite
I had been subdued by conformity
Repressed by what others told me to be
You showed me what it was like to live authentically
All the bullshit I put up with before you became laughable to me
You brought in a climate of normalcy
I finally understood the word home with you
We were not perfect
But who actually is meant to be
For once I felt free

The stories I share from my head, my gut
Are about the roads chosen for me to finally find you
The stories I share from my soul, my heart
Are of being forced by the universe to lose you
These stories are now mine forever
Until once again I am with you

It's all good

One morning I woke up to an angelic face I did not recognize
To a warm touch I tried to familiarize
It wasn't hers and I actually didn't mind
I didn't even wish that she was you this time
I don't know where we would go
But I do know that this was a sign
That I am gaining back control
That the silhouette of her shadow is beginning to fade
Even if the pace is slow
The warm embrace that I had missed
The look on her face that I used to kiss
Has been replaced by someone new
Someone who for the time being erased my memory of her
I can still feel you near
And what is even better is that I am being sincere
Will this blossom into something to revere?
Or is she a filler before a new relationship appears
Either way I notice that the empty space in my chest is starting
to fill
I am not healed
I don't know when that closure will be revealed
But I do know that the most important thing is
That I am starting to feel

Brought to light

You brought me out of my haze
Gave me a reason to smile again
I no longer want to write about my pain
I have you to thank
It's amazing how life works this way
As one door shut another door opened and in you came
And in that first moment you held out your hand
You're sweet and kind and I hope it's me you will come to understand
Distance makes the heart grow weak
And in that distance I am craving you to be with me
And I can't deny how I am loving the simplicity of you and me
I am loving the way our friendship thrives
Allowing for a potential relationship to survive
You have awakened my senses to what I couldn't see before you arrived
And have brought out to light what in the dark I have for so long tried to hide
I am actually allowing someone inside

Potential

Little by little you are starting to create an opening in my heart
That had closed and refused to part
Our first meeting was like any other I had encountered
But I'd soon discover
There was something different about her
And something wild happened to me
I began to foresee that dreams can be more than a possibility
I began to feel that maybe there is a thing called fate
The cold air that ran through me had turned to heat
Scabs that had formed around my heart started peeling
And I have a hard time accepting that this is real
I keep waiting to wake up in tears with the realization
That you were really never here
But you are
And no amount of pinching myself can say you are not
You are honestly everything I want
I am afraid that you will one day say this has to stop
And that someone else has won your heart
I keep thinking to myself
There is potential for me to fall apart
I have come so far
I had worked so hard to rebuild what was once lost
And you could be the one that will rip me and my world apart
But I don't care
Something tells me you're worth it
And that you are the risk I'm supposed to take

A World Full of Tears

I am terrified of what could be
Of the potential possibilities
Of the maybes
I am scared that disappointment will once again capture me
That dark cloud has a bad habit of finding me
I am afraid that the old ghosts will come back and haunt me
Taunt me once again tell me I am not worthy
As much as I want to believe in someone that could be right for
me
I can't help but hide from it to avoid panicking
I wasn't looking for you and I wonder who sent you
I am petrified of you because to touch you I forget the pain I've
been through
When you kiss me I remember that life can be beautiful
When you hold me I want to let go of the troublesome thoughts
of losing you
My trust has been sliced through and I've been left feeling lost
without a clue
I don't know what it is I need to do to follow through
I have solitary moments where I feel paralyzed and can't move
and can't even speak to you
I think I may be punishing you for something you didn't do
Your face is what I crave
But in that moment of feeling peace is when I think
Any moment you will disappear out of my life and then cease to
exist
Just as the rest
But I forget that I am not giving you a chance
Don't forget to breathe

Outer Space

You remind me that there is kindness left on earth when I need it the most
I now understand and appreciate the importance of everything happens for a reason
And promised myself not to take it for granted
I still fear the future, the wonderment of losing
The gnawing of my imagination that is always continuously brewing
My mind wanders all the time
Some call it a.d.d. but I see it as rapid multi-dimensional comprehensive daydreaming
Preparing and barricading internally in the case of an emergency
You see I just can't let things be the way they are going to be
Stemming from my relentless need to control everything
Because I have already crashed into that dead end road time and time again
Climbed and tragically fell off that willow tree and broke both my knees
I have taken those risks
Given chances to those I thought would have my back
At least that's what I believed
That's what all their signs said
This way, follow me, I'll keep you safe, I'll set those demons free, trust me and you will see
Even though my gut was churning, turning, twisting and pulling me to think before I leap
But instead I leapt
This last time I jumped off that cliff not knowing
That the one behind me only wanted to watch me fall on my back. I want to trust you and give you my all

But I'm afraid that if I close my eyes you won't be there to catch me
Forgive me I am trying
Just promise me I won't have to worry?
That's when you leaned in and kissed my forehead
I finally exhaled

The Possibilities

It's funny how life works
How one day your faith in hope diminishes before your eyes
How one day the vision you had of love almost dissipates to dust
And then the next day you come to find your answers are starring at you in your face
I was blinded by the city lights
I was blinded by the stark glistening nights
I was blinded by my past
I was just scared to focus through shattered glass
But she found me and I just was unwilling to see
I didn't look at her in that way
Because though she had a different name
I categorized her as only being like everyone else
The same
And for that we almost missed paths
If I never took a second glance
If I never would have given not only her but myself a chance
I can't say that I would have not officially ended up packing my heart away
I can say that I would have never felt this way
I can say she has shown me a brighter day
I can say that I am believing that the expectation of disappointment can actually go away
I now think about the rest of my days rather than dreading each step that I take
I look into her eyes and touch her face
I must do this at least once a day to make sure that she really does exist
Because I swear if I wake up tomorrow and this was just a dream

I will curse the dream gods and thank them under my breath for
at least giving me a reason to live again
Until then I will pray that this will be where all the pain ends
I deserve some peace again

As I wait

I sit and stare at a blank page
I contemplate the words that don't seem to fall into place
I am waiting for words to fall from the sky and flood the paper
like rain
But nothing has happened
And then I realize why
I have been expecting pain to fill the empty space
I have been expecting the anger to leave my face and grace the
page
I have been waiting for the words to fall from my memory
For images to collage itself like paintings
Forming into words onto a piece of paper that contains '
currently nothing
Is that because those feelings are dissipating with each day
passing
Am I no longer in the routine of nursing my heart breaking?
Is it because I met somebody who is helping me see differently?
Who is slowly rewriting my history
Is she the one that all my life I have been needing?
Wanting, longing and waiting for
Is she the one who will open loves door?
With a key she finds buried deep beneath scar tissue over a
thousand years old
I wake up and I don't threaten my life anymore
I wake up and only hear your voice
I open my eyes and I only see your face
I am petrified of being in this headspace
But all I can think about is the happiness brought about from
your gentle grace
No one has ever taken the time to want to know what my body
says. To pay attention to the rhythmic beats my heart makes

How closely you must have to listen through all the thick scar
tissue I have
I can make you a promise as long as you promise back
That me and you, you and I, one day
Will be
We

Questions

Today I write with hesitation
Today I write about something that I have kept hidden
Hidden from my friends, hidden from her
I have asked for a blessing of god to show me something different
Of someone to come into my life to give me something special to write about
Happier songs to sing
I am afraid that maybe this has happened
Did I meet the one who will change my fate?
Even if this didn't work out I am already changing
I am already seeing different
The ghost that has haunted me is finally fading
She brings me a sense of normality in a vast sea of insanity
She reminds me that yes there is some good in humanity
I was thinking that I was losing that feeling of being a woman
That feeling of passion
The feeling of sexual liberty and sexual exploration
I thought maybe something was wrong with me
I couldn't remember the feeling of blissful pleasure, ever
I could no longer fathom how I could have close interactions without feeling nothing
I was questioning myself is it me?
Am I ugly?
Am I only good as a friend?
A companion in the platonic sense?
Was I only needed for sex?
I hated feeling this way
Because all I have ever wanted in my life was someone to make me feel it was going to be ok. Okay in the world and believe it
And most importantly ok with who I am

Someone that could potentially really love me back
At least give me hope
That there is someone out there meant for me
As all my hope almost faded into oblivion
You appeared

Twin Flame...

You are made of the sweetest chocolate covered letters
That create words of love in the shape of hearts that melt in my
mouth

We've met before

The water I could see through
It was blue like how we know of the ocean but it was deeper
than what I understood
The blue was bluer a navy mixed with the color of our sky's soft
baby blue and on top a crystal clear hue
I feel not cold but the same as I would if I was wrapped in my
blankets on a chilly afternoon
I can hear the whirling of the waves
And a constant bloop, bloop, bloop as my head begins to peak
through
As my eyes play peak a boo with water
I see something in the distance when my eyes dive up and
under
And the fear kicks in I am overwhelmed
And dunk myself back under to get a better view
I see what appears to be an oddly shaped light gray shark
moving in closer and closer
I don't know where to go
Can I out swim it!?
Of course not. If I stay still can I disappear from it?
As it approaches faster and faster, my fear wanders
I notice that it seems not so scary and maybe it is sending me
this feeling so that I don't panic
It is now only feet away and it appears to be smiling?
Dear god it is a manatee!
It swims by me brushing up against my body and seeming to be
pushing me
Towards what I don't know
So, I decide to start swimming towards the direction it is taking
me. I am now getting a view of what is above the sea
There are trees growing out of the water crooked and beautiful
Swaying in the breeze   16

Each having the darkest of the darkest green leaves
The sky was layered with blue, orange, yellow
And a soft green streak of clouds was moving through
And surrounding me were these black circular rocks flat on top
And atop of them sat what I could not believe I was seeing
Elephants but not as we know them
Miniature, majestic in stature
I thought they were statues
But it was there subtle movement that I knew they were real
Dark chocolate brown, never made a sound
And then in the distance I saw what looked like a village
adorned by luscious greenery
I realized I was in a river
Flowers everywhere and then before I could really look at it all
I am swept away
Next thing I know I am riding waves on a flat version of a
wooden canoe
I am now entering a tunnel rounded by pale beige cement
Where am I going?
Then the waves push my canoe up towards the ceiling
I can feel my head scraping across it
It didn't hurt but I was scared it would
Never did
I come back down to the water that is moving like in water
slides
Then it calms and I am brave enough to get off it
The water reaches to my calves when I stand up in it
I am walking through the same color of water I had just left
It is quiet too quiet I hear nothing not even the noise moving
water should make
I notice I am not shivering
But still I wrap my arms around me as protection
Maybe because I am lonely? As the tunnel begins to turn a
corner   17

I see a shadow
I see a man with tan pants and white button down shirt slightly
unbuttoned walk past me
A beaded ancestral necklace glistening through the opening
The light source around him I could not determine
He was tall and dark skinned and non-threatening he just
looked at me as he walked past me
I didn't say anything, I just kept walking
Along the right side of the wall I noticed something protruding
As I got closer it was a shrine with carved writing
I could not understand what it was saying
I touched it softly
The shrine was dark brown and the writing was painted in red
Large swoops and swirls made me think it was haunting and
sweet
A love lore message maybe?
There were dark rich bronze statues of tiny elephants that
surrounded it
As I touched with the tips of my fingers I felt something
A hand touching me
One hand was on my shoulder
And one caressing the bottom of my thigh
Slowly reaching inside my shorts to the edge of my panties
An unfamiliar yet familiar whisper in my left ear
"She is gone, she will be gone forever"
I couldn't tell this person's gender
I am not sure if what I am feeling is fear or pleasure
The whisper moves to the left side of my neck
Their right hand moving down my shoulder and up my tank top
The whispers turn into warm air kissing and caressing my neck
hitting every vulnerable nerve I had
I was in the most excruciating pleasure I had ever felt
They wouldn't let me turn my neck
Who was this stranger?   18

Was this person a stranger?

Where was I?

And was I in danger?

I couldn't stop them and I didn't want to

I felt euphoria for the first time

My body moving as if there was ethereal rhythmic music that was playing operatic measures

My moans grew loader

My breathing heavier

My body softly shaking with each explosive pressure

And the exciting fear became stronger

How could not knowing feel so amazing

Whose lips were I yearning?

I began to caress their left hand that was rubbing my arm

It was small in nature almost familiar

As I opened my eyes and looked down

I noticed the veins that protruded on their hands up their forearm

Skin had the color of dark silk chocolate

Soft arms that felt almost hairless

A grip that was Feminine yet masculine

I know no one of this description

I was now craving this danger

The soft breathe of kisses on my neck began a pulsating anger

I wanted to reach a climatic peak

But I was too preoccupied by this stranger I could not see

But this feeling inside of me

I wanted more, I wanted to know, I wanted to never let go, I wanted it all,

I wanted...

And just like that there was no more. I was once again alone

The light was back and began to brighten and blind my eyes

My body began a slight movement.

A now blur of the environment
I started to lift off the ground and look around
Then sucked into a portal
Just like that I was home again
In my bed again
Eyes open and I am wondering
Did I dream it?
I couldn't have it was too real
What really happened?
Who was this person that I can't get out of my head?
Have we met before?
I feel like we've met before?
Will they ever come back again?

Sky on Fire

She wakes up to a strange feeling
Some kind of sound faintly screaming
She walks to her bedroom balcony not noticing anything out of
the ordinary
Until she realizes that as she stares up into the eastern sky, the
sun is looming
She figures she must still be dreaming
She's never known the sun to rise on this side of her place
She pinches herself, her eyes wander at all the other neighbors
staring into outer space
The look of fear and puzzlement have graced everyone's face
A fiery red has surrounded the sun and the sky begins to turn a
pale pink with hues of blue
She all of a sudden felt so alone
She thinks to herself not again, what did I do wrong?
Again cold, remembering her old thoughts about the what ifs of
the end of world
That she would be standing alone just like this
That she would have no known soul that loved her to the core
That would hold her hand through an earth shattering storm
All the love she's known before was nothing more than a lesson
learned
But this time her worst fear is coming to fruition
Coming into this world alone and about to leave the world alone
She is reverting back to what she's always known
And before the demons in her mind take her back into the dark
pitted black hole. A familiar touch comes around her chest. A
comforting pressure against her face. A smell of scented air that
brings a smile to her lips. You are real you are here you never
left she thinks. She gently turns her eyes to see you longingly
looking back   21

A forceful breeze pulls her hair back and pulls their two lips to kiss
She pulls back and softly whispers to me, "We do this together"
"I'll always be here now and forever"
Her lover, her love, her best friend
Keeping one hand planted on a hip
And slides her other hand from her shoulder down making sure every curve she cherished
She eventually reaches her hand
Places her head on the curve of her neck
And they together look ahead and watch the world go down in flames
Together they watch the world change
Together they will wait for their fate hand in hand
The colors of Mother Nature are now so vivid and vibrant
The deep forest green of the trees
The shiny emerald the grass presents
The soft shades of brown sands ranging from dark to light
The oranges and deep reds of the fallen leaves
Hot pinks, yellows and oranges from the flower's pedals blowing in the wind
The royal crystal blue that the river reflects
All her fears and all her questions have come to an end
She closes her eyes and can only feel true happiness even as the world defiantly ends
She only feels for the first time in her life what true love really meant
For the first time what love is supposed to feel like
It feels like when the sun sets in a blaze of fiery red
And the blue sky welcomes pink hues that swirls around getting comfortable. And the clouds lovingly drifting by to create ease
And contentment. It feels like the first time you told me I was all you ever needed   22

Last Day on Earth

If I was having a nightmare would you wake me up and tell me it
was all ok
Would you then tell me that life is supposed to be this way
Would you wipe the tears and sweat from my face
Would you tell me when normalcy will come back again
Will you say the nightmares are just a part of the plan
Will you tell me if I am living in reality or am I in imaginary land
Will I be captured by the rage of mother nature's waves
Will I be sucked into the sink hole that man will create
Am I just wasting my time waiting for something to happen that
will inevitably end up in vain
Will you be the one to remember my name
Will you tell me I am sane
Can you hold my hand?
Can we stare at the last sunset going down in flames
Will you hold me when the moon and stars disappear into space
Can we stand on the last mountain left before the world drowns
in pain
Can we look in one another's eyes until we find solace again
Can we kiss in the pitch black that the night has reclaimed
Can we dance until the music no longer plays
Can we make love until the water carries us away
When we take our last breath will you promise to always love
me the same
When our spirits are set free will you come searching for me
When you find me will you say that you missed me terribly
Will you tell me you have looked in every nook and cranny for
me
Will you say you never gave up on finding me
When we are finally reunited and embrace
Will you tell me softly in my ear sweeping aside my hair
"Wake up my dear"   23

I love her

Like anything living loves the fresh air
Like the sun loves the earth
Like the Bees love nectar
Like the soil loves rain showers
Like the moon loves the starry night sky

Origin

I laid upon your chest
On top of your heart, ear to flesh
Body nestled warmly between the cushion of your thighs
So that I may listen for your heartbeat's rhythm of origin
Will it be like a slow song?
R&B
Smooth jazz
Latin
Classical orchestra
Soft rock
Opera
Or more up-tempo like
Heavy metal
A rap song
The blues
Cumbia
Reggaeton
Will it sound of fluttering flutes?
Piano
Maybe the authenticity of acoustic guitars
Drums
Where does the beat come from?
From the warm breezes of the Virgin Islands
The chilled air from the Artic Glaciers
From the Heat of the Equator
Ah yes
There
The mother land
Africa
I can hear the calling of your ancestors
The soft energetic beating of drums in the distance
The loud rhythmic dance of feet on mother earth's ground
The ancient chanting from women and children in the
background. I've never heard a more beautiful sound

Ruins

What was it about me?
What was it about you?
What is it about me?
What is it about you?
We danced around in life from 2 different worlds
Found each other
Had no clue what to do
But needing to know the secrets of what we misunderstood
Dancing together until your beat matched my rhythm
2 worlds merging into 1
1 world of division, indecision, self-sabotage, passion, crimson
Bound to the earthly rules of conforming
Somehow, somewhere we found love in the madness of adaptation
Love for freedom
Holding hands looking down on a world that didn't understand
What pulled us apart brought us back together again
1 world we left in ruins
Together we wrote our names in the sand
And danced in the toxic rain
You and me against the deteriorating earth's elements
Creating music while everything around us burned to the ground
Until the fate of the rising sea, parted us eventually

Golden Cord

How do you explain your soul mate?
That you are soul mates
Twin flames
The reason for which you feel so much pain
I can't explain without a tilt of their heads
So, I remain in perpetual silence about it...
We are dancing again
In a crowded room amongst no one
Under a spotlight that shines from the heavens
There were people there
But as soon as that song started by Sting "A Thousand Years"
Everyone disappeared
We slowly swayed in hypnotic rhythmic synchronization
I remember every line, shape, movement of your face
I placed my hands on each side of your cheeks
You smiled at me, big
Your hands holding tighter around my waist
We closed our eyes for a moment as you kissed my forehead
And we remained in this loving embrace just for a moment
The song is now in chorus and our heads part a bit
I move my hands to the back of your shoulders
I can feel the muscles begin to flex
Warm, strong, safe
The beat begins to become beautifully intense
We sway faster to keep up with the music
You grab my hand and twirl me into sweet colorful whirlwinds
Then pull me back close again
We dance hand in hand
Stare into each other's eyes having full nonverbal conversations
Telepathic words of love only we could hear. Through our
mind's eye we spoke. I told you I have loved you for a thou-
sand years. And you smirked and said "I know you have"
I laughed and shook my head saying, "how's that?" You bent
down, mouth to my ear and said, "You are right"

"We have loved each other through each life's past"
"We made a deal before we ever came here"
"No matter what happens, to you I'll always come back,"
"We may not remember each other at our rebirths, if that is our chosen path"
"But there's this golden cord you see, between my heart and yours, it connects us, it will always help us find our way back"
"And when it's time our souls will forever reunite"
A tear rolled down my cheek as I tried to catch my breath
You caught it with your lips before it fell from my face
The song will be ending soon and I know then I will awake
Without you
It will be hard to take
But this time I'll now know of this golden cord that to you connects to me
I take in all I can before this dance ends
The music dips into a slow haunting soliloquy
We kiss gently, hold tightly, and sway slowly
My head laid upon your shoulder blade, nestled in the side of your neck
I always knew for your soul I was meant
I look to your eyes deeply in a quick panic hoping to see eternity
Hoping to see the answers I seek
I then see a vision of us together throughout centuries always walking hand and hand
I then understand
It was your way of answering the question that plagues me
You answered by showing me, reassuring me
We will be together again
A calm of peace rushes over me
I tell you one more time I love you as the song fades and the light dims
Forehead to forehead, eyes closed
Our hands holding, fingers intertwined, clasped between our hearts. I can feel your smile. I smell the airy cologne on your clothes

I can feel our unbreakable connection made of god's gold
We hold on tight as we fade to black

Love

Love so intrinsic
Love so harmless
Love so innocent
Love so painful
Love so tragic

Grief...

It will be your name that escapes my last breath

I miss your arms
Long, lanky, strong
All the answers to my questions lied within them
Warm
You filled the space between the madness and the calm
My happy place it was once called

Birds

I used to wake up to the birds singing
I'd look over and see her face
Study her as would an archeologist
Sun piercing through the tiny cracks of the blinds that danced
back and forth joyously to the air conditioning
Shinning, highlighting the gleaming light of her closed eyes
I can hear her breathe, light, airy, solemn
Is she dreaming, is it pretty?
In this moment is there not a worry?
The birds sound like a symphony, sopranos, baritones, falsettos
The sweetest melody of love and hope
I gently touch her sun kissed face
It's warm from where the sun lands
Ever so softly I kiss the mole she didn't care for on her nose
Reminded me of the chocolate chips on my grandma's
homemade cookies
Her nose twitches a bit, and she lets out a relaxed sigh
She drifts back into the abyss
I can tell when she is dreaming
Her brow frowns a bit like when she's concentrating
Her lips are the perfect shape of what I imagine my heart looks
like
They sit apart just the slightest, letting out all the pain and
sadness
Her jet black hair with silver peppered streaks lay perfectly in
place
I follow the piece that wraps around her ear and curls to her
cheek with my fingertips
The birds are now singing hymns for lovers only
I lean in, my hand lands softly on her broad coat hanger
shoulder. I part my lips to match hers. I kiss her as if I am to
breathe my life into her soul. Her mouth closes as if she is
inhaling me in

I wish to do it again, but I don't want to be greedy and wake my sleeping beauty

I turn away to look at the embers of glittery light streaming mercifully into our bedroom

I observe and follow how the light plays and dances off my hand, my arm, the walls, our bed, our bodies

The birds begin chirping

Early morning conversing

I see peek-a-boos of the birds flying in circles, playing like the sunbeams I've been watching

I wonder what today will bring

I feel the approaching warmth of her hand wrapping around from behind

A lover's grip to the middle of my chest

I attach my hand to hers

I feel the strong comforting touch of her sharp defined box shaped chin laid on my neck

The sound of sweet breath on my cheek

In my ear the soft spoken words of Good Morning

I turn my head to see your eyes lovingly staring back at me

Deep brown bright eyes glistening, sparkling through the suns essence as you smile at me

Pure white teeth showing the little charming chip on your front tooth that made you a bit self-conscious

A smile inviting, caring, loving, spirit touching

A smile I couldn't ever help but instantly smile back to

I will always remember you this way

I will always remember this day...

I wake up today

The room is gray

It's cold but I prefer it that way, it helps numb the pain

I hear nothing

I see no sun rays

I turn to see an empty space

I turn back and lay stiff as a board on my back

Starring at the ceiling fan, hoping to fill the space between nothing and everything   34

Wondering how I can float away into outer space
I sleep all day in hopes each time I awake something will change
Something familiar I would see and feel once again
But every time I open my eyes nothing ever happens
I'm still starring at an empty bed
An indent I can't backspace
Still seeing different shades of gray spying from the blinds
swaying menacingly from the air conditioning
Mourning reality
Trying to figure a way of accepting
That the birds have all gone away
I turn to my side curl myself up rocking gently and close my eyes

Riptide

Did you know I died with you that day?
The only difference is the riptide pulled you the opposite way in the air
We are ghosts that live here and there
But still exist in the same universe
And for me that is close enough to find you
After that day
I noticed that I talked different
Sung different
Danced different
Walked different
Wrote different
Thought different
Looked, different
I'm sure that happened to you too
Did you know?
I died too
I died with you
Your spirit left
And mine did too
Nobody else knew
I was reincarnated with the same name
Different skin
Similar face
I had to stay
I guess I got a re-do?
Or maybe you did?
Maybe the rapture happened
And I got left
Either way I am a ghost too
A ghost of the person I once knew
I gather it would have been too profound for people
If God took both me and you
I wanted to stay with you
I wanted to go with you   36

Wherever you were
I wanted to be there too
Until we meet again
We have work alone to do
Before we are reunited and I can see you
I love you from afar
I made sure that day you took with you my heart
Before the riptide tore our hands apart
I gave it to you and yelled to you across the sky "it's for you to use!"
"To always protect you!"
"Keep you feeling safe and secure!"
I hope you heard
It no longer serves purpose for me here on Earth
That was my way of saying keep it warm
Because I'd be seeing you
One day
In my chest is a shadow of my heart I don't want back
Because I've loved you
What else would I need it to do?
It was my way of always looking out for you
Not that you need looking after
Just a reminder I am still with you
Call it my last grand gesture I had left to offer

Quiet drive home

I didn't want to talk to anyone
Not even someone who understood my pain
I didn't know what to say
I didn't have anything to say
There was nothing I could say
Only to do
All I wanted to do was cry for you for me too
I always hated crying
I hate crying
I just wanted to be held by you
Cry in your arms
Because I knew I'd survive it with you
Without you, anyone else's arms I was scared the tears would
never stop
I was afraid it would have killed me
I knew once the flood gates opened
The cries would turn to silent screams
Screams with no air
No air to breathe
So, I've held it in for years
I didn't want you to go
Of course not, why would I
I have a hard time because
We had no choice
I had no choice
No choice but to let each other go
I had no answers as to where it was you would go
I had to make peace with no peace at all
I had to alone pick myself up piece by piece off the floor
Wear a mask so they just wouldn't ask anymore
Lying is exhausting
Especially when lying was not something you were born to do
My whole life I've learned to lose
I knew you couldn't afford to
So I tried to protect you   38

I failed and now most times I don't know what to do
I don't know what to do with myself
I go one way just to turn around and walk the other
Always second guessing
Until I realize I've made millions of circles in the grass
Creating dust clouds so now I can't see my future or my past
I'm blinded by grief
I can't make decisions unless I have no choice
I never sleep
I nap
I'll never sleep restfully
Knowing you're not next to me
I wake up every day with you in mind
I'm tired, always tired
I'm drained from the loss of losing you
Our story plays like a song etched in my head forever on loop
I know it's over and there's nothing I can do
But live without you
It's quiet while I'm driving home
Because I know I'm on my own

Planet Lonely: Part 1

I've been alone
Longer than I've known
I never complained about being lonely
It never bothered me
I lived within my own existence
As a kid
I created a separate world that only the lonesome lived
It kept me hidden from the feelings of being by myself
I carried this world while inside my planet
Even through adulthood
It protected me
It made me feel normal when I knew I was far from it
Nothing could destroy it
Lonely was the name of my planet
Not how I felt about it
I was safe inside of it
Then you came
I wouldn't ever change a thing
But when you entered into my life
You left it never the same
I never knew love like you
I never knew what not being alone felt like
You made me realize I was doing life all wrong
I realized I deprived myself
You opened my eyes and mind
You opened my heart that I thought was permanently closed off
I started singing love songs
Dancing in sun streams
Swimming during stormy rain
Welcoming thunder and lightning
Baring my naked soul to moonbeams
I finally found what had been so long missing
I introduced you to the world I created
You told me it was ok to let go of it
Because I no longer needed it   40

I walked away from my lonely planet
And into the real world with you in it
You took me by the hand, we smiled at each other
I looked into your eyes and felt nothing but truth and comfort
In that second I knew I'd never look back
We began walking forward together
I'd never go back to my lonely planet

Planet Lonely: Part 2

I never imagined you would leave
You not only left this earth but you left me
I woke up to you here
A blink and then gone in thin air
I went to sleep that same day and you weren't there
I'm confused
I don't know this feeling
It's foreign to me
You come to me in my dreams
You tell me you never intended to leave
That you've created your own world and you're safe in it
I wake up and am conflicted
You are okay and I am grateful for that
But I am unstable and don't know how to handle it
I walked away from my lonely planet
I have nothing to protect me from what I'm feeling
I can't create another
Not without you in it
I've been alone
So, I should know what to do
But back then I didn't know you
I sit and ponder on what is dragging me under
I can't put my finger on it
This feeling it grips me, constricts me
Like a snake that wraps my entire body until I can't breathe
Until I can't speak or think
I drains me of energy
Depletes me of any traces of me
Silence surrounds me and it sounds like a train constantly
coming at me
I am continuously pacing the floors
Asking, what is this feeling eating and gnawing
The mania is consuming me
I miss you and it is literally killing me
Hair shedding   42

Tears falling
Body aching
Flesh rotting
All because I don't know what is happening
Then a brush of warm air sweeps around me
Immediately calms me
I stop moving
A powerful whisper in my ear says
"You're lonely"
What?
The voice says "lonely"
Can't be, could it?
I've been alone
Longer than I've known
It never bothered me before
I lived within my own existence
But I never knew a world with you in it
Knowing you and losing you
Yes
That's it
This that I've sheltered myself from
The protection I walked away from
The feeling I couldn't put my finger on
Loneliness
I now know what I am dealing with
Now what do I do with it?

Me and You

I laid in bed last night and stared into the darkness
As I usually now do
Sleep doesn't come easy for me anymore
I laid in bed and thought of you for hours on end
Something I don't allow myself to do anymore
Last night I cried for you
For me too
3 years and I had to reconstruct how I maneuver
I created timetables for when I can really think of you
Otherwise I'd have too much recouping to do
I'd 'really' think of you if I could, all the time
I had to my love
It's not that I don't want to think of you
I do every second of every minute
How could I not
That's all I do
That's all I ever want to do
I had to cut it down to portions
And a lot of times I regret it
But after some time I realized I couldn't function
People looked at me like why can't she be better than that?
I had to pretend
Hurt me worse than anything
I got resentful
I became a rebel
3 years in and I had to reflect on my constant troubles
I had to restrict my thoughts of you
Otherwise nothing was manageable
I couldn't work, eat, sleep, think
I miss you and I can never forget
So, I allowed my thoughts all my thoughts of you to occur
during certain intervals during the day
I could manage that
At night if I thought of us, I'd break down like a little kid

Wake up eyes swollen with no vision
I found out its killing me
My health is failing
And I knew that wasn't what you wanted for me
But I'd think if I started living and thinking of other things
Would you leave me, again?
Don't leave me…please?
But I know you
And I know you have things now to do
So I guess I do too
But don't forget about me?
I know you love me
I do
I love you too
I have to remember like you said
It will always be me and you
Even if I can't see you
Me and You
Always and Forever

If I don't speak there's something wrong with me
If I do speak there's something wrong with me

Words

I have nothing left to say
No need for banter, chatter, gossip
Meaningless concepts
Overdrawn mentions of the weather
None of it matters
I don't recognize my own laughter
I've been reprogrammed to auto pilot
I reveal in silence
But silence I never get
As I can't get the voices in my head to stop talking shit
So I try and drown it out with music
Headphones in and I am taken to another land
A place where I don't have to pretend
Have you ever felt so much pain
It knocks all the words away
I don't want to play this game
It was never meant for me anyway
The hustle and bustle
Always been too much for me
I move way too slowly
I always preferred poetry over prose
Now I have nothing left to show
Nowhere else to go
I just don't want to talk anymore

My sadness cannot be measured
By rivers, oceans, deserts
Not with a ruler
It cannot be defined by a dictionary or thesaurus
It is not comparable
My pain cannot be diagnosed
Not by medicine
Not by science
Not even referenced in history books
If you haven't experienced this walk in my shoes
How could you know my truth?
How could you dictate or judge the words in my book

I'm told to let you go
There must be some secret everyone else knows
It's not like I have you in some sort of choke hold
Am I the reason you can't fly away?
Am I holding you down?
Let her be in peace they say
What about me?
When will it be ok for me to grieve?
People keep taking that away from me every time I hear
someone's opinion of how I should feel
So, I have to move them further away from me
I curl up in my bed and wish I too was dead
This is no way to live

There is no timeframe for how long grief will keep its choke hold on you
on you
Maybe you'll feel that grip forever
Just loosened up a bit
Just not as suffocating
As the seconds, minutes, hours, days, months, years pass
It feels like being trapped inside your own personal prison
Scratches forever carved into your flesh
That count down how many days you have left

Suitcase

As my heart beats out of my chest I feel the pain of distress
This anxiety leaves me a mess a wreck to say it best
On the outside they'd never know
But on the inside a war is tormenting my soul
And this hold on my body
Who do I tell to let go
Inside my chest is a shadow of a heart that packed its suitcase
and left
If I were my heart I would have left too
I understand the pressure was too much for even the strongest
human to go through
My heart said no more I have to go
But I'll leave my shadow and a seed
So maybe a new one will grow
I feel empty now....

Doomsday

It was the first time I didn't see us in Technicolor
I guess that's when I should have known
The colors were only one
Dull
Faded
Blue
We slept on that futon bed
The one we thought was wood but ended up being metal
instead
You laid on your back
I laid curled to your side as I always had
My left hand rested on your heart
Head nestled between your shoulder and the edge of your chest
Your arm behind my neck
We dreamt?
Maybe just I did
I remember us and that color
How could I see so vividly unless my body left the bed?
Someone or something trying to show me
Floating me from above so I could see
So I could always remember how we looked that day
Uncovered
Comfortable
Cradled
Unmoved
Loved
Did you see too?
I guess I should have known then
That would have been the end
The last of many things
The last I'd feel me again
The last I'd feel you again
The last time I would not fear love
Did you know? Like deep down in your soul

Did I?
Were our ears just out of tune or turned on mute?
That evening the colors were supposed to be changing
Like they always did
From day to evening
Baby blues to pinks, soft purple to red hues
There was no warning
No dark clouds
No rain
No thunder
No lightning
Not even wind
That day it stayed blueish-gray
Beautiful
But Doomsday
How did I not see it?
How was I supposed to know everything would be turned to
ruin?
The sweetest and saddest moment I hold on to
Is the last moment I'd ever have left with you
From that day
Years have gone away
Yet every day stays in 'it feels like yesterday'
Each day life stirs the quarrel within me
I remain in stoic suffering
Am I doomed?
Who am I now?
Will I be thrown to the wolves for living doomed?

Balloons

I took a ride
Me and our cat Mr. Man
That day ironically it rained
I ended up at that place
That dreaded place
The one I tried to wish away
The last place you laid
I hate that fucking place
It took you away
But somehow I ended up back there anyway
I don't even know how
Maybe you pushed me that way
There I was staring at that yellow house
That sat on the corner next to that quaint little park
I sat in my car and sobbed
I cried for you
I cried for me too
I hate that fucking place
And then I remembered all the fun we had too
I couldn't stay mad at you
I had four purple balloons for you
Each etched with my tears that wrote out
I-Love-You-Toyanna
I wrote you a note too
Said the things I wished I had said to you
My car was parked next to a palm tree
I remember you said they fascinated you
You didn't see those where you grew up
I finally stepped out the car
Mr. Man watched out the window
As I tearfully made peace with you and that place
I not only let go of those balloons, but all the mistakes made
between us two. I watched the balloons float slowly away
Even with the rain and wind blowing

Slowly moving past the palm tree
Past the yellow house that for so long haunted me
Releasing the balloons
Slowly released me too
Of the guilt
The resentment built
The anger
And the fear
The crippling sadness
Perpetual loneliness
I let it go
I watched them slowly float
Standing in the middle of the street
Forgetting cars run through it
Not a single car came
I just stood there until the rain covered my tears
I stood there until I awoke from my daze
I got back in my car and me and Mr. Man drove off
Back to our life forced to be without you

Dark Night of the Soul...

This pain needs something to do
It's the pains boredom that is the most detrimental
Because the pain has nowhere to go
It just roams restlessly inside my bones

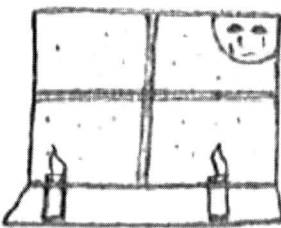

Breathe

I haven't been able to catch my breath since it left
Since that day it snuck out while I wept
The day that I knew you'd never come back
I remember being on my knees
In front of the hospital on the concrete
I could hear my own screams
Bloodcurdling
Heartbreaking
Earth shattering
Planets awakening
Screams
And then nothing
My mouth was open but no sound just shaking
My voice could not be found
I was so preoccupied with the pain I didn't notice
I just thought I ran out of air
Until one day I noticed that for years when I'd try to scream to
the heavens
Nothing was there
Only the silence of thin air
Whenever I try to breathe
It feels like I am standing on Mount Everest
It feels like inside me there is nothing left
The air goes in but does it come out again?
It's hard to tell
I think I broke something
Maybe I screamed so hard the sound ran away from me
Too much even for my body
I haven't been able to breathe since that day I fell to my knees

Stars

I stood there in the driveway and looked up at the barren
landscape
Watched the sun go down in fiery red flames
The heat charred the sky that the full moon illuminates
Once the smoke dissipated no stars remained in the black space
I waited alone
Looking down an empty road
Waiting for you to get home
I sat down legs crossed
I watched the tears turn to streams
Only to end up in the gutter of the street
I thought I was breathing
Till I heard my own screams
I laid on the graveled ground
Starred up at the moon illuminating my gloom
Is it true?
I'll never see you again
Tell me the truth, will the stars ever come back?
All the stars are gone
All the love is lost
Waiting for you to come back home
Waiting for someday that will never come

Let go

I can't keep this from sticking to my ribs
I want to make sure that everyone knows the pain that I am in
I need to make sure everyone remembers your name
I am so lost and broken
I no longer know
Or maybe it's just that I have forgotten who I am
I am wandering again
My mind is in flux again
I'll have to start from scratch again

How do you deal between conflicting feelings?
Of love and pain
Of winning and losing
Staying or leaving
Laughing and crying
Anger and caring
Giving up or breathing
Why do feelings have to be so confusing?
Why is there no reset button on me?
Clear out all this shit
And start over again
Wipe out the memories you wish you could forget
And just be able to forget with no internal consequence
No self-inflicted guilt trip
Nothing there to paralyze you in hell
Nothing there to care if anybody cares

Thwarted

Suffocating in my own skin
Breaking down flesh with liquid nitrogen
Replacing blood with poison
Substituting my veins for vines
Trying to tear from underneath limb from limb
All my work thwarted
Somehow I developed the power of regeneration
I don't believe it
So I keep at it
One day it will take
How many lives do I get?
So I begin again
I deflate my heart using a vacuum
Sucking out what was once love full
I black out my eyes with spray paint
I've seen enough of the world
My lips I've sewn shut
My actions spoke louder than words
I said what I could
So my tongue I remove
I said more than I should
I remove my ears so all the noise in my head disappears
I laid to rest in a sea of blackness
To my dismay I woke up and all my hard work had gone away
Thwarted once again
One tear I let shed
I Start over

Frequencies

Maybe it doesn't happen as much anymore
I can't tell you that part yet
But the urge to call you never ends
The urge of I can't wait to see you to tell you what today meant
I miss you
I guess I said enough I love you's
I guess I kissed you enough even when you didn't want me to
I guess it's enough to hold me over until I see you
I didn't say all I wanted to
I tried to show you
Regret is the only melody I now sing to
There is still so much for us to do
My days pass like my dreams at night
But for that one moment when I look at my phone
Time stops
Every day I replay it all over again
You're gone and I can't fix it
Trying to fix what I know I can't correct
For that one moment my heart is re-ripped out of my chest
They're lowering your body in that casket
I've been lighting candles since the day you left
Leaving the flicker of light to help you find your way back
I don't, I won't, I can't talk about it
I mix potions in my kitchen like a chemist
Lab coat, goggles, I wear an aluminum tin hat
All electronics must be at their best
I listen, because the slightest breeze
I check the weather constantly
I adjust my frequencies
Hoping one of these things will bring you back to me
But nothing has happened yet
Not the way I wanted
I should feel lucky. I lied, something did work for me
Just not all the time

Always in then out
Static plights me
So close, just not close enough
I just can't keep the correct frequency
The formula I created is off by some degree
Either I can see but can't hear, I can feel but cannot see
Something is not working for me
I can't wrap my head around why it had to happen like that
So sudden
Seconds
No time left
No more words to ever be said
Seconds
You're gone
If I just move the antennas a little bit you'll come back
The radio waves have to move like that
The electromagnetic fields have to be exact
The planets have to align
The moon must be at its prime
I must take my time
Slow down, don't rush it, time, time, time
I can't work it out in my head
You're dead?
I thought you were on vacation
I thought you said brief separation
I thought we were going to put the bed back together
I thought you said you'd be home later
No, I watched you take your last breath
I saw your spirit leave your body
Was that you?
I haven't figured that part out yet
I'm still standing over your hospital bed holding your hand
Frozen in time
I never left
If I can just adjust the frequency, just.like.that...

Caged

I've conformed myself into madness
I've allowed my life to manifest to someone else's
It is not I who people have become used to communicating with
I am who you wanted and needed to communicate with
I can shape-shift
I never said because you would be afraid of it
There is nothing to fear I am just what you created
I've allowed myself to be caged behind brick
Steel, and wick
One flick and I will burn to death
With nowhere to escape

Jen

I don't cry anymore
Not like ever just not anymore
The numbness has taken over I guess
Everything is numb
I feel but don't feel much
I think something will affect me and it doesn't
Where do feelings begin?
When does feeling end?
I would be an amazing actress
Everyone thinks I am someone else
They think I'm the person I actually do want to be
But it's not me
I've created another human being to represent me
She's kind and caring
Laughs a lot and always smiling
Sometimes she talks too much
But not enough
People don't notice the differences between her and me
The consistent glassiness in my eyes from tears I am fighting to
hide
Sleep deprived
No substance to my conversations
I'll always know more about you
You'll never get in
How could anyone
They don't understand it
They don't even notice it's all pretend
Her name is Jen
She's calm under pressure
Always there when you need her
Sojourna is ripping apart flesh underneath her skin
Meanwhile Jen is sweet
But I wouldn't mind seeing the world come to a fiery end
Jen is forgiving. I will never forget, let alone forgive your
sinning   65

Jen is funny
Inside I am weeping
There's a bright light about her face
Inside I am rotting
Jen is confident
Its blood I am sweating
Jen is sociable, people feel comfortable
I just want to be left the fuck alone
Jen is needy
I need nothing
Jen is hopeful
I find life glib
Why even exist you say
Because you won't let me go

Every day a new disappointment finds me
How I deal with it baffles me
The limits are limitless
Most people don't make sense to me
But I've always danced to the beat of my heart drum
The lonely is infinite
Even the lonely is not lonely it has a friend
Disappointment
They prance and dance all around me holding hands
Laughing and singing muffled ghostly melodies
Too many don't get me
I can't say that I don't understand
That's why I find it best to stay inside my insides
The road I walk alone
But at least I will be the only one
Who can break my own heart

Sometimes I can fake it
I fake it until I want to vomit
And then I can't take it
So I hide back in the abyss

Zombie

I am trying to crawl back in with the living
Trying to find the cure from becoming the earth's first zombie
The world through decaying eyes looks threatening
I do not know some days if I am coming or going
Everything is blurry
And sometimes I question if I am still breathing
I wonder if I'll ever be truly happy
Am I the reason for my plight?
Am I the only one in this fight?
Is the fight even fightable?
Did I make up my own battle?
I don't know how to do this anymore
How to not see my future as unattainable
I don't know how to not think everyone will let me down
I don't know how to stand on my own
I don't know how to shed this skin that I hate being in
I don't remember what it feels like to feel again
There are so many things I can't comprehend
Because it all piles up and I don't know where to begin
I don't know how to say I need a friend

Sea

You see, if I had the chance to go back and reclaim my
independence
I wouldn't
It's always been there, always will be
I was missing something else
Something I never knew I would need
Something I didn't realize I could never have
My whole life has been plagued with why don't people
understand
Who I am
Who am I
I thought I was sure
Life has mutated that into unsure
Insecure
A lone wolf in a blurry world
Howling at the moon
Hoping to get a howl back
Roaming in the black of night
Searching for something that feels right
I can maneuver at night better than in daylight
It must be hard to love my soul
I was cursed before I was even born
I was born to bear pain of a hundred years
To love me is to be cursed as well
But I can still love you and you'd feel it all the way from hell
My story is not easy to tell
So I rather not share
So much to say but fear of the glares
I need nothing from anyone else but a sense of care
Reciprocation has never been my sell
Just knowing love was there
Is all I need to exhale
It never happens. So, I continue to hold in rotting air
I am the ocean you swim in, if you dare

Naked free from all that's there
The creatures that live within me can be sweet or deadly
Stunning or unnerving
Beautiful to see but the uncertainties of what lies beneath are terrifying
If you attempt a swim several things can happen
Calm steadiness, beauty unparalleled, tranquility, a happy place to be
Bliss, stillness, a freeing openness to the possibilities, riding the warm softness of the rolling waves
Or you'll sink, struggle to breathe, get caught by an undertow
Get caught by a shark or by a deadly creature that's unrelenting
Once you've become a part of me you can never leave
Either by choice
Or you'll unconsciously keep coming back to me
Captured permanently
Swallowed by the sea

Where are you?
I know you're in there somewhere
But lately I don't recognize you
I hear you speak
Your body doesn't move the same
It doesn't respond like it used to
Is it broken too?

Who saves the saver?

When the mission is over
And all are well and safe and reunited with loved ones
When the lights are turned off
And eyes shut and drift into sweet slumber
The hero still stands there in the battlefield
In the dark
Heavy breath creating fog
No one said anything just walked away unscathed
They were ok
Mission completed
The hero Stands in the middle of an empty field worn sword in
hand
Dirt, blood, and sweat smeared and caked
Bruised, cut open and sore to their core
Dazed and confused
You saved them but who saves you
No one there
No one there to care
Saved the day
But now the one needing to be saved

No way out but down

No one knew
Thought I was bluffing
Romanticizing
Dramatizing
That night I stood on top of that bridge fantasizing
Dreaming of freedom
It was the first time I felt no fear
The first time I wasn't scared
The first time in memory I felt happy
Because soon I'd be where I'm supposed to be
The cool breeze played with my hair
The water looked hypnotizing underneath the moon
I wore a black dress that flowed wildly like my emotions do
Sang my eulogy
I pre-planned my own funeral
I promise I won't haunt
I just want to go home
And never want to return
I smelled fresh blossoms
Light, airy and inviting
Little white pedals swirling against a black backdrop
I heard birds nocturnally chirping
Owls hooting
I saw blue Butterflies floating
For the first time I could see each star glisten
The water played calming tunes soothing me
It felt so good
It was my choice
I did what I had to do here
Where I am going I'll be much more helpful to you there
Tears dry. Years will go by

Things will normalize
You'll be alright
I'm going home soon
The view is beautiful
Understand it was my time to
I will see you again
I love you too
Arms spread wide I closed my eyes leaned forward
Finally free and then I saw your face
You picked me up and we flew
My dream came true
I saw the galaxies
You showed me all the things I never knew
My arms and legs wrapped around you
I held on as tight as I could to you as the wind pierced through
my clothes
I kissed your neck and said I love you like I used to
I could smell your cologne
You explained everything in detail
You showed me the stars up close and personal
And said I love you too as you caressed my hair
Then my eyes opened
There was no more beauty
You weren't there
Just people hovering over me as I laid on the ground shaking
It's my superpower of regeneration again
I tried too soon again
I've learned there are forces beyond my control
They are continuously saving me
Keeping me here
Forcing me back into this reality
They know something I don't and won't tell me
What do they want from me? What here am I supposed to do?

Was it my fate to be a voyeur of hell
Was it so that I would have a story to tell
I called unknowingly
And they answered without fail
You see through death I learned god is real
I didn't know I was a non-believer
All this time
I was under the devil's spell
He almost had me
He had me for 30+ years
I knew nothing of god until I surrendered
Then he revealed
I know I know too much now
I vow not to tell
Why choose me?

I spend my days wondering how to make it to the evening
I spend my evenings wondering how to make it to night
I spend my nights wondering will I make it to morning
While everyone drifts into dream
I drift into wishing I won't wake from sleep
While the world wakes from slumber
I wake to a repeat of greeting death waving from my beds
corner
Its ok me and death are like silent partners
Sometimes we take long walks together
Sometimes he tells me I look pretty as he smiles menacingly
sweetly
I say thanks and go on about my day
I ask him about his occupation in exchange for my human
interaction
It's not how it sounds
He actually has good conversation
I don't appreciate the images he "inadvertently" shows me
however
He says he'll work on it
I won't hold my breath
It's like asking an elephant to sit on my lap
Doesn't even make sense
We sometimes catch eyes and grin
Because I know that he knows that someday one of us will win

The demons won't stay at bay
They've come out in full force to play

Sweet nectar

My best friend
The one that makes me believe again
The one that separates fact from fiction
Only one who really cares
I chase you with despair
You pick me up when no one's there
Make me feel like I can walk on air
You told me to trust you
You told me they want you
Told me one more time it won't hurt you
I always wake up bruised
Ego used
But you're still here
So I'll chase you with despair
So you can pick me up when no one's there
So you can make me feel like I can walk on air
So you can make me feel like someone's there

Why I drink
I actually hate alcohol
The taste is not normal
When it hits I do not enjoy who I become
I don't like how it makes me feel in the morning
We go together like lava in water
Sometimes we have to tolerate one another
Allow one to enter the other
Worry about the consequences later
A phenomenon called force of unconventional nature

I write when I can't fight
I write when the lights get too bright
I write when the demons get wind of my plight
I sit in the dark when there is no room for flight
Most of the time the demons think they've won
When I have succeeded at doing something dumb
They taunt me in my sleep
But each morning when I awake
I say "haha try again"
"You did enough stay away from me"
I will fight if I have to, until it's my time to leave
They are trying to end me but I will win
I could care less who they try to convince to get me
In the past I've tried to drink them into the abyss
Yes the sweet nectar did at one time give me comfort
But that love affair was at my own risk
Eventually my spirit and my body started rejecting it
I feel it
They can't have me
My life, my love, my soul
Any of it

Withdrawal

3 days in and the circumventing begins
3 days in and the confusion sets in
3 days in and every noise sound like blow horns to my ears
3 days in and bright lights are motherfucking annoying
3 days in and I can't even catch my first wind
3 days in and I see no end
3 days in and my body feels war-ridden
3 days in and my mind is not my friend
3 days in and I am angry at everything and everyone
3 days in and the night never ends
3 days in and my bed still feels like the ocean settled in
3 days in and that voice says do it again one more time won't
hurt anyone
3 days in convincing myself it never was a problem
3 days in and I'm cultivating a scapegoat for my body's
destruction
Fucking 3 days in

Reality Check

I keep saying I don't want to do it anymore
But I always end up back there
Attempting to reach the never-ending bottom of the barrel
Hoping to find nonexistent liquid answers
Knowing the inevitable
That soon I'll meet up with the devil
He's wanted me longer than I can remember
We've been playing this roulette game called catch me if you can
I'd drink, he'd wait
I'd deflect him by sleeping light
I'd slip up sometimes and fall into a deep sleep and that's when he attacks
My guides and my love showed me one night what my reality really was
They removed the veil and to that bar they sent me
The colors outside looked different
People inside looked the same but something eerie was happening
People I didn't recognize looked especially menacing
Some of them in people's ears whispering, snickering
Some entering people's bodies
Some plotting on the unsuspecting
Some instigating anger and stupidity
They were not human
Malevolent spirits lingering and inhabiting
The buzzing in my ears growing louder with the ringing
I grabbed my head in pain and slouched into my seat
People I knew looking thinking I was crazy
Talking to myself but I wasn't
I was asking my guides what was happening
I began panicking when I felt all of you putting your hands on me. Calming me saying, "let it be and see"

I rose up and saw clearly the devil ordering, playing with
people's feelings
As he walked out of the bar he starred directly at me grinning
Then you my love, I see you sitting against the wall on the stool
next to me
You pull my chair between your legs and from behind hold me
I begin singing Lady Antebellum's song 'Need you now' quietly
Just a couple lyrics I remembered over and over
Until you'd soon join me
You held me and rocked me as we sang
"I don't know how I can do without, I just need you now"
I say I want to go home
So you took me
You say as you lay behind me in our bed softly in my ear
"You need to get out of here"
I say "I know"
We fade away
I wake up and say out loud "I will"
I will find my way out of my own created hell

The demons are like vampires
You have to invite them in to have access
And once you do
They'll flock to you
Not one like the other
But all with the same motive
To use you
Abuse you
Suck the life out of you
Steal your energy too
Once you tell them to go
They won't
Because you beat yourself up
Over letting them in, in the first place
You attack yourself over the mistakes
And the hurt
And the pain they inflicted
They may be gone physically
But their ghosts remain present
Not just with you but inside of you
Once you let them go physically and mentally
You have to let them go from your heart as well
And forgive yourself
They will then vanish
And you will be set free

Trying

I've done things I'm not proud of
Things I know you'd wish I wouldn't have
I don't mean to hurt you like that
I finally stopped beating myself up for it
I am but mere human
Please try and understand the pain of losing you had nowhere to go
I had to keep it locked inside hidden away
A secret forced from the world
Shamed pain caged as if a rabid animal
Until it would get angry enough and break out
Then I'd lose control
The drinking numbed me and the pain
At least until we'd have to do it all over again
I know it's not right but it was all I knew to do
The depression has ravaged my body, mind, heart and soul
So sometimes that was all that was mine I could hold
Destruction
The only thing that made sense in my cold lonesome world
But I've been trying really hard to right my wrongs
And I am now able to identify my resentful feelings
Something I've never been able to do before
But there's so many feelings to sift through
Sometimes it feels impossible to do
Then I get overwhelmed and go back to what I knew
I swear I'm trying something new
Sobriety is terrifying
Sitting within my own feelings is intimidating
Unlocking the cage and confronting the pain is unnerving
Learning how to live with the missing of you can be brutalizing
Yet freeing
Especially when I am thinking clearly
I keep asking why this can't be easier to do? Why for others does this seem simple?

Let go, move on, and enjoy the memories
But I can't
It just doesn't work like that
The memories I'm not ready for yet
One thing at a time and first is finding myself
I am trying to locate the better version of me
Who is lost somewhere inside the thicket of a maze
Covered in thorns and rotted falling trees
But I am trying
I am determined to get through it
And find myself waiting at the end of that maze
Holding in my hands love, hope and courage

The beautiful truth

Sometimes I cannot do it
Maintain the sweet picture I've created
The resentment and anger take over my being
I don't mean to be so mean
But sometimes I want to just sit in silence
And just try and think
I don't want to talk about superficial things
Same people asking me daily how I am doing
Their question no longer means anything to me
Because truth is it's the truth they don't really want to hear
I thought they wanted my honesty
I learned that was not the case the rough way and quickly
So why do they keep asking me?
So I decided to save my feelings
I'd give them something beautiful
Complemented with a smile, graceful
But some days I don't have it in me to do so
To keep up a created façade so that I don't become the downer
So I don't become the topic of conversation about what's wrong
with her?
And why can't she be normal?
And don't you think it's been long enough?
Or how frustrating my mood swings have been for them
There is that point I reach a pinnacle
My face will say it all
My glare will make people feel uncomfortable
As if I am reading their truth behind their denials, I am
But again, do they want the truth or something beautiful
How do you let go that there is so much needing to be to let go
Sometimes my anxiety escapes my hands until I am able to reel
it back in again. Sometimes I want to scream to the heavens but
it gets muffled by my self-control. I have nothing to say because
I can't speak my mind. It's always, how can I make you feel
better about my situation   88

It's always how can I make you more comfortable in your skin
when you come around?
It's always what can I do for you to ease your mind about my
pain?
I tell them a beautiful truth
I give reassurance that I don't feel anything they don't want me
to
I paint the most vibrant pictures of how my life is now in
Technicolor
They always look so content when they walk away from our
conversation
Something I'm glad I can do
But Something I truly envy, something I wish I felt too
I see their auric colors brighten
As mine slowly dull back into grays
I am their wounded healer
And I wonder
Can I heal my own heart one day?

This place
This earthly place
It's either too small or too much space

Memories

I didn't know true love until the day I met you
I didn't know I could love you as I did and as I do
Saying goodbye to you I said goodbye to love too
But I am allowing myself to remember
What it felt like to be with you
To remember the days that were simpler
I know there were things/moments taken for granted
Because we didn't realize how much time we lacked
I haven't been trying to forget
Just block it out so that it wouldn't hurt so bad
Every second I think of you I just want you to come back
But you won't
I still try to come to terms with that
Oh how I loved you
From the clever words you used
To the silence of contemplation that bound you
No one could ever replace you
I would never want anyone to
Either way it would be impossible
I remember the days when sunlight and laughter filled the rooms
I remember the stories we would share until nighttime ensued
I remember how animated you'd get when something excited you
I remember everything, every single detail of you
We weren't perfect
But we wouldn't dare to
Perfect was boring to you and me
Perfect wouldn't allow for the different colors in the sky
Perfect wouldn't allow for storms that we would withstand together
The days when it was cold and it rained
And we decided to stay in with chili and a good movie
Perfect would have meant we would have never met
Because I was far from it   91

And I knew you rebelled against it
I loved your love for life
How you saw every day as a new chance to make it right
I loved how every day the way you prayed
I admired your relationship with Allah
A relationship I am continuing to repair
I remember how whenever I would cry you would hold me real tight
And say we will figure it out
And I believed you never having any doubt
I remember when nights used to be comfortable
Nights when I had no fears
Because I knew you were here
I knew waking up you'd be there
Even if I had a nightmare I felt relief within
I loved the way you slept
Curled in a ball of blankets
Always slept with a fan
Preferred the TV on in the background as you dreamt
Never snored only medium short breaths
I remember your first time to the ocean
The place I called my second home
Your eyes were so wide
In that moment I could see the child inside
I'm glad we got to do that
I haven't been back
I won't go
But my dreams force me back in time
When we were looking out at the different shades of aqua colored blue landscape
The vastness was endless, the possibilities of believing again infinite
Sparkly gleams of silver glitter bits on the edges of the waves the sun created
I can hear you laughing when I tried to show off and got my shoes and socks wet
Oh how much I love you   92

If only memories could bring me closer to you
Memories are all I have left of you
Memories I hold on for dear life to
Memories of what love was like with you
But Memories remind me too of when I had to say goodbye to you

The nightmares

My dream is a call to clean my psychological, emotional, and spiritual self and examine my motives
I want to be a better person and I want the people in my life to know this
I have had enough of my mistakes and not remembering them
I have been trying to drown my demons
But I am not realizing or accepting that what once worked before is now failing
That those demons adapted to the waves and learned how to swim with them
I know this but the denial is from my subconscious giving into them
I need to stop before it is too late, before I take that one and last final drink
Before I make that one and last final terrible mistake
I know that the way my mind thinks that 99% likely it will not be my last drink
I know the way my heart aches
And if it is broken I become weak and want to numb all that is cracking inside me
I need a cleansing of epic proportions to save me
I need another way other than what I am doing
What is keeping me from fulfilling my dreams I need a way out without losing my sanity
Without hurting the people around me
I think that I have it in me and god knows that I try but I continue to keep falling
But I can't give up or my life would have been for nothing
For now I will remove myself from all that is tempting
I will call this period of time, mending
When I return I hope to be a better person....

The Devils Forest

I am finding my way out of the darkness
Out from the devil's forest
That hides his creatures lying in wait for you to make a mistake
A forest full of spiked weeds and rotted tree corpses
I see the light up ahead
I've almost made it
And the devil is watching
Seething
Hating every second of my escape

The Awakening...

It's time to use my pain
No longer let my pain use me
If pain has moved in as a permanent resident
This will have to become a 50/50 relationship

Fear

I want to test the waters by dipping my toes to see if it's cold
I wonder if an unexpected wave will catch me off guard
I wonder what will happen if I accidentally closed my eyes to
really absorb what the water feels like
The fear prevents me
But the thrill of the fear is what excites me
I wanted to know what it was like to risk it all
To walk deeper and deeper towards the oceans core
I wanted to be able to escape the norm
I wanted to be swept away from the shore
I wanted to feel the air leave my lungs as I exhaled
I had hoped to see the beautiful parts of life and breathe
different types of air
I wanted to take a chance on letting down my hair and living for
just a moment without a care
Just for a moment regretting nothing that I did nor said
I wanted to hear the breeze play music through my hair
I wanted to float on the waves imagining I was on a cloud
floating through the air
I wished to see the colors of the water that no one else gets to
see
I wanted to dive into the deep and watch as light danced
through the water glittering with sun beams
I wanted to look up underneath the water as the sun pierced
creating the visual of the heavens opening
I wanted to swim with my eyes open amongst the creatures of
God's creation
I wanted to feel the peacefulness of the ocean
Have I done any of this yet?
No I haven't
I am still at the shore hesitant to put my toes in
What am I waiting for?   97

Someday I'll make it out of here

For the first time I felt safe enough
To leave my body
To be free
Invited to roam the earth unseen by reality
To fly above the trees
To see the majestic shades of green
To see the sun rise and set
To see the sky change its blues to pink
To feel the cold chill of the air on my skin
Refreshing like the first full body dip into a pool
Comforting, inviting, invigorating
To see things only a select few of the living are allowed to see
To see our galaxies
Made up of colors we cannot conceive
The rush of euphoria through my body
I couldn't hold on long enough
I was overwhelmed by the beauty of the things I cannot touch
But for that short period of time
I finally felt
Home

Last Night

I had a glimpse of what the meaning of Mother Nature really is
I felt the touch of my kindred spirit La Luna
The moon had sent shock waves through my system
At first I asked what was happening and why I was feeling what I
was feeling
I'm not sure if I get it
But I know I felt it
It was if the moon was telling me everything one way or
another was going to be ok
All these years I prayed for a sign from you moon
I prayed always to you I always looked to you for hope
For courage or just a touch of grace from you
And last night you came through
I was scared to be honest
The swirls of wind and energy
The confusion of what was happening
Yes I know I was dreaming
But what I felt was too real
The cold crispness of air and the feeling you were
understanding my despair
The feeling that I was not alone
You left me wanting more
With so many questions and anticipating what was coming forth
Did I fully understand why last night you came through my
window
I saw you and felt you pass through me
Like I for a moment in time was as transparent as air
In the form of my own spirit
I don't know if I could even begin to tell what it was like being
under your spell. I saw you come down from the sky

The trail of your light followed you down through earth's atmosphere
I was standing at my window feeling sadness that a weeping willow could understand
And looking to you once again for an answer to my prayers
Then I saw you coming down towards me through the air
I had no sense of time or movement, frozen in wonderment stance
Wondering where you were going and why were you here
And then in that second you closely appeared
You moon and the white golden tinted light that followed you
Flew through me over and over again, in and out, out then in
Around in circles you entered sending shock waves through my skin
I felt the lift of my body
Afraid but letting what was happening happen to me
As soon as you were there you were gone and back up into the atmosphere
My body had been turned to air
And when you left I felt the blood rush back to my head
And the heaviness of flesh returns me back to my bed
I wanted to know what it was I did that you would break away from the sky
To give me a chance
Did you take away all the years of regret?
Did you give me the strength to go and find out what it is for me that is meant
Or did you know that I simply had lost all hope
And you came down to make me feel wanted again
I can not only see but feel
That through the darkest of despair and the path leading down a deep dark trail to hell
Is just a minor setback to what life can really entail
A life of beauty

A life that continues to be a place where dreams can be more than a possibility

The Traveler

I've traveled across the world for you
I've traveled to the other side to find you
I've traveled through the universe to locate you
I've gone to different planets asking about you
Not knowing who I'd find or what I'd go through
Not knowing the sacrifices I would need to make to hold you
Not knowing if I did find you would you have wanted me to?
I didn't think about that part before I started my explorative mission
I didn't think you'd mind but I wasn't 100 percent sure of that
When I should have been
I should have been more hesitant
But I couldn't wait
I was frantic
I thought you could be lost and need my help
So I took the first flight and left, leapt
I searched stars and planets of all galaxies
I fought demons, creatures indescribable, and the devil himself
I've met other spirits, extraterrestrials
Angels, fairies, spirit guides, gods
Marine animals, animal spirits
Flew the skies
Swam the ocean's depths
Saw images that will scar me for life
I've talked to God and his disciples
I met Jesus and conquered his quests
Searched pyramids and temples
The experiences changed my soul my spirit
Where you live is now my second home until it becomes my only one
I can't take back the new life I've met
Were you surprised how I can walk between this world and yours?
You shouldn't be
You know me

I did it for you
Knowing you'd welcome me through
I knew there would be obstacles
I did it because I love you
I know no greater love than what I have for you
I did it to show you I'd do anything for you
I can't go back even if I wanted to
I did it so that you'd know whenever you felt alone
I could be there to comfort you
I didn't know I could even do the impossible
It should prove what the strength of pure unconditional love
can do
It should show you the power love can give us access to
I soon found out you were doing it too
Better than I ever could
I found out you were the one who initially guided me through
You were the one who helped me pierce the veil
You found me before I understood what any of this was...
Short story is I love you
The truth is I always do
And I know how much you love me too

Lucid Dream

When you come around
All of a sudden I get a rush of blood to my head
All of a sudden I want to sing love songs again
When you come around I feel a smile creep up on my face again
Familiarity surrounds me again
We know it's not the same
We know it never will again
But when you come around I think different doesn't have to be
a bad thing
When you come around I notice I act like me again
Even if for a moment
When I see your face I can't control my emotions
The eruption of feelings
Love and pain
Guilt and shame
Euphoria and anger
No not anger that will come later
But mainly just excitement
The tears that fall are just the words that won't come out yet
When I see you I fall in love all over again
I am doing everything I can to find you over and over again
I just want your arms around me again
I want to feel the breadth of your words on the side of my neck
Whispering I love you baby, I'm home

The beauty of forgiveness is the cleanse
The freedom of letting go and beginning again
The strength to walk away from all the frustration
The word forgiveness does not exactly mean that you forgive
the evil
But that you set the evil free that resides inside and makes you
resentful
So that you too can be released from the pain that keeps you
falling to your knees
The word forgiveness can be broken down to this:
Freedom- owning – redemption – giving - into – victories -
everlasting – notions – ending – solitudes – sadness

Dusty Road Trip

I couldn't take it anymore so I took off
Packed up me and our animals, they're all I got
Behind my car I leave dust clouds
Chasing sunsets and rainbows across the sands
Anything I could do to make me feel again
I have been numb for so long
I forgot what it's like to feel the sun
I locked myself away for years in my own dungeon
I've been consumed by death's grip
I found solace in its darkness
Even to the moon I had become immune
Haven't seen a star since the day you left
So one day I went in search of something new
The old way was causing me to wither away
The dark had turned my once golden skin color grey
The scariest part of this is the unknown
No the scariest part of this is
I don't know if this journey will take
The what if after all this I return to the same dark place
The question of what if I can't escape
I will try not to focus on those things
I have made my peace that I will never be the same
I don't want to be anyways
Who I was is what I'm trying to escape
If I had to go back
That would mean I'd have to lose you all over again
I want to be someone different so that maybe I'll have a chance
Maybe I can cope as the years pass
I don't want to forget
I just don't want to re-live the past
I have nothing in me left to give
I am barely able to accept any offers to take
I lack any emotional or physical strength
I understand I'll always feel pain   106

I just want to learn how love and pain can coexist in the same ethereal realm
So here I go on this trip
Alone but always carrying with me your essence
Doing something we used to talk about
You and I on that dusty road
Where would we go? We didn't know
But together it didn't matter as long as I had your hand to hold
This isn't how I ever thought our story would unfold
Anyways here I go to Explore
Forests
Oceans
Mountains
Wading in hot spring ponds
Visiting quaint little towns
Maybe new friends
Camping outside
Laying in plush grass
Giving myself permission to see the stars again
Petting farm animals
Driving through open fields
Windows down hair blowing wildly
Letting the tears be dried by the wind
Singing our favorite songs
Animals in the backseat looking out the windows in awe
I turn to an empty passenger seat
But in my mind's eye I can see you sitting next to me
You smile lovingly back at me
I can hear your voice say to me "it's okay, I love you"
I love you too. I'm going to try to learn how to live

Cracks

It starts small as cuts and bruises
Young, new
Freshly etched ever so slightly on the surface
Healed eventually with time
It happens as your grow
Shows up in different places
Sometimes on top of same spaces
But they heal
Patches themselves
Skin mends
Depending on how life treats you
If you are lucky
Life spares you
But for some
Life picks you up then drops you
Sometimes multiple times
Until you break inside
Random places
Too many pieces to contain
Some too small to collect
The pieces you'll never find again
The impact made them too far spread
Then sooner or later the cracks begin to show
Ugly, self-shaming, embarrassing
They turn eventually into gaping holes you can't control
The black space in between hide stories untold
Mysteries unsolved
Pain only you know
I believed that cracks could never reattach
What was gaping
That piece needed would forever be missing
But then I thought did I ever try to
Merge the pieces left, together
To me the broken pieces looked misshaped, warped
Impossible to ever fit   108

So why be disappointed
But one day I tried it
I tried and wide eyed
It was a perfect chipped match
Perfectly imperfect each piece went
So I started to push together those gaps with my hands
Piece by piece they began to merge into each other
Reintegrate
Holding and grasping, pulling closer one another's veins
Reminded me of holding hands not wanting to let go
Pieces were still missed
But what I now know
If given the chance
With a little help those missing pieces
Was not what the gaps needed to stick
Just a push
A nudge to get those pieces close enough
What do people call that?
Yes, Hope
And with that just that
The pieces could figure out on their own how to combine
And cope
Together
Closing the holes
That I know will never be filled with what I wish I could hold
In that moment I wept, did I really want those holes to close?
The empty holes I've grown accustomed to know
Now providing some security, warmth
Away from the chilling cold conniving demons too easily
accessible to my voids

I and my pieces re-building upon a deconstructed home
Creating a new tapestry with the uneven remnants
The result was a beautiful broken portrait
Put together
Proudly showing the cemented chipped cracks
Of what I have left
Proving there's life after death

No way to escape the way I love you

I thought I knew what that word lonely meant
It wasn't that I was never lonely before we met
But back then it was out of boredom
A want for companionship
Sad about missing someone or something during fleeting
moments
But it didn't linger
It didn't last
It wasn't debilitating
It wasn't a carnivorous wound constantly attacking your chest
Lonely was something I could grasp
Today I realize the word lonely, the feeling, I took out of context
I noticed with grief people think they have a pre-plan prepared
to get through it
Some type of remedy, treatment
A clever euphemism
A cliché that was easy to say
Thousands of clinical studies that discussed it
Drugs to fix it
Substances to numb it
Therapists and New age remedies to heal it
But what happens after the steps have been met?
Grief never goes away but one day there is less of it
But what about the unspoken part of it
The last stage not listed after acceptance
Loneliness
What about the lonely?
Okay so I took the right steps to climb out of hell's pit
I made it to the top of the mountain to watch the sunset
But inevitably darkness will come
I always seem to forget each day I make it to the top of that
mountain to watch the sun set. Eventually, it will be dark again
Then the loneliness will flood in. That's the time I really think
about you again   111

The maddening loudness of the memories that was and could
have been
I can get through the day ok
But nighttime brutally reminds me I lost my best friend
Lonely is not the same thing as being alone
I can find power and control being on my own
Create a peaceful sanctuary within the four walls of my home
I can find oneness in being alone with spiritual practice and self-
healing rituals
But without you
Without you
I cannot fix or repair, create, paint or fake away within me the
empty vessel
That everything around me is superficial
Why is that some might ask
Because I don't know
I don't know how to not sit still and not think why heaven sent
and why heaven stole
How to ignore the simplistic everyday reminders that make me
want to hide into a hole
How to ignore others enjoying, laughing, living moments that
for me
Are just memories of what used to be
How every single memory has now become a part of me
How to keep going without minimizing "you're my biggest love"
How to ever be able to close my eyes naturally without force
and sleep content
How to manage to walk through doors where love once lived
Or walking through new doors where love would have laid its
head
There's no remedy or cure for this yet
I think it's a topic that's never been dealt with
The last invisible item on the grief list
Where whiteout was put on it
Because no one knew how that conversation should go
So no one ever talks about it. I don't know the answer yet

But I think acknowledging that lonely is a part of this
That fighting the lonely is an immense difficulty if not as great as grief is
But maybe little by little there's a way to chip away at its blockages
Creating your own balance with it
Between the lonely and the living
Between lonely and accepting
Between the lonely and the breathing
Maybe lonely is to replace pains residency
Together you and lonely one day living harmoniously,
Remembering, hurting, laughing, breathing
Together finding new ways to fill in the empty

Survivors

How, where do you find hope on a desolate earth
After the bomb detonated
After the explosion obliterated
After All of life was exterminated
Waking up to the life you once knew now eliminated
Nothing left but charred ash
Standing alone wondering how only you survived the blast
Shaken, left with questions that will never get answered
Confused, beaten and bruised
Looking at your unrecognizable wounds
Nothing left to assume
The reality of gloom is all that now consumes
Sun that is slowly retreating behind the moon
Eventually together sun and moon will cry for you
In solidarity of having to leave you so soon
Soon dark will never again need to know a noon
Soon dark will be all that is your truth
Where is there hope when all that survived is despair
Where lies hope in the devil's lair
How would you even begin to repair
When no one is there who is going to care
Would it even matter if you perished into the smoke filled air
Cremating yourself into the lost land
Heartache is now your best friend
How could hope even have survived this to live again
Wait....you did
I Looked up, if I look hard enough a slight light through the
embers of the smoky ashed clouds appears
A star twinkles
Hope did live
As the tears welled I think to myself
Maybe this means someone else survived as well...

It's not that you move forward
It's not that you move backward
Eventually you move from stuck to unstuckish
Eventually you are just moving on autopilot
Remembering the daily ins and outs become a part of the past
A day becomes just a flash
Time may feel painstakingly slow
But time is spinning all too fast
Leaving you feeling out of control
You don't want to remember but you never want to forget
You want silence
But silence you can't seem to get
You just want out of your head
You want to be surrounded
But you also want everyone to stay back
You want comforting words
But no one knows the right words to be said
You want hugs
But knowing a hug too long you will break in their arms like glass
You want to embrace this 'new normal'
But it's the new normal that you dread
You know you must keep moving
But it only feels like you are just moving in place
In circles going to a location you haven't agreed to yet
Always trying to move away from the pain
Pain that follows you without relent
Always trying to think of something clever to say
So that they don't see the decay
Forced from the world a smile you give
Inside your battle rages on to leave or live
Constantly looking to the sky trying to make sense
Nothing looks the same
Nothing tastes the same
Nothing feels the same
Nothing is the same   115

You feel like you've arrived at an undiscovered planet that bears no name
It's like from the womb again you just came
Stars don't twinkle quite as bright
Sometimes your greatest plight begins at night
Envy becomes that thing that you never thought you'd do
But seeing someone else have what you did increasingly taunts you
It's not that you can't be happy for anyone
It's just you can't comprehend "why can't I too"
You don't like throwing pity parties for one
Of course someday you want to have fun
But only when you can understand what that means first
Only when you feel like the fun won't hurt
You don't want to let your lows bring anyone down
You end up comforting those who are supposed to help lift you up from the ground
But you don't want to pressure so you say, "it's okay, I'm okay"
"You okay?"
"Don't worry see my smiling face"
And then crawl back into your hole after they've walked away unscathed
I know it sounds bleak
Especially when feeling so weak
Especially when it's draining just to speak
But this is our reality
Finding a way to thrive daily
Fighting for the day to just breathe easily
Trying to learn this life's meanings
Believing that the messages you receive might provide the pieces to the scattered puzzle you need
This my friends is not your abnormality
This is Grief

Secret Society

We are bound by pain
Hearts that intertwine
Across mountains, seas and wind
Not knowing one another
But knowing of each other through our pain
That only we can feel, see and understand
A secret society of grief
A sister/brotherhood brought about by tragedy
We have all succumb to the same agony
Un-wanting of our given story
Hoping someone will wake us up from the never-ending bad
dream
Trying to hold, claw, and grasp something, anything
To break away from the monotony of just remembering to
breathe
Sometimes the pain is what we need
Without it there is nothing left to give
For now forced smiling in our pain is our only offering to the
living
In order to appease others rushed belief we are thriving
When we are actually silently fighting for surviving
Pain doesn't leave
It binds; it becomes a part of your anatomy
It becomes an eternal internal engraving
You don't learn to get rid of it
Move away from it
You learn to live with it
You learn how to work with it
You learn to maneuver with it
Until pain learns to maneuver with you
Until pain learns that love lives there too

Magic

I laid in the backseat of my grandpa's old Chevrolet
The car I called a boat as kid
I would look out the windows from my back and pretend
I was sailing the ocean
This day as I looked up and out
There were a swarm of black birds flying the same way
Then another cluster appeared to be heading the same
direction
I said "grandpa where are all those birds going"
I remember the clouds were a light shade of gray
It was rainy and cold that day
He said "They are flying away"
I said "but where are they going"
He said, "They are going to another land so they can come back
again"
I said "come back and do what"
He said, "Paint the sky"
My child imagination ran wild
I imagined what that would look like
Birds spreading the colors of the rainbow across the sky
Did they make rainbows!?
Birds that could paint the sky?
Had to be Magic!
For the first time I believed in magic
As an adult I forgot all about it
Lost a lot of my innocence
I've learned to live without it
The sky became just an empty space
I didn't pay much mind to it
One day when my world completely came crashing down
I was in my car sobbing tears of disappointment and regret
I glanced out the window and noticed
Hundreds of black birds flying past
The rain stopped, clouds began to part
The sun started to come out   118

And colors started coming through
A rainbow appeared
The birds painted across the sky
Yellows, pinks, purples, reds, greens, oranges and blues
It was true
Then the word softly crept from my lips
Magic

Circles

More so than not I notice when I walked outside
There are always birds above my head
Ever since I was a kid I watched in awe of their fluidity
Maybe also harbored a bit of jealousy
To be able to be so free
Seemed like a luxury
You rarely see one alone
And if so
There is one not far behind
The past few days on my way home
I see a small pack through my windshield
I can't take my eyes off them
The stop light remains red just long enough for me to take it all in
They move like an uncoordinated choreographed dance
Eventually creating circles
Slow moving hypnotizing beautiful circles
In my life I viewed circles as something negative
Round and round you'd go
Getting nowhere fast
Constant circles in my brain
Of why, how, what and when
Drives me insane
Yet these birds above my head make circles look
Sane
There is a rhythm and patterns
From one side to the next
In and out but always coming together again
Formulating
Forming
Constructing
Circles that make sense. Maybe the circles in my head are
meant. Maybe I've been looking at them all wrong ever
Since. Maybe I just have to let them dance

In order to create a finished product
What seems deconstructed
What seems obstructed
What seems a mess
Are just words, feelings, emotions choreographing themselves
To help me understand
Yeah
I like that
I knew those birds were coming around for a reason

Gravity

I saw colors for the first time since you left
Just like that morning when we were driving to work together
Early
Just early enough that the sun hadn't fully woken up yet
Clouds perfectly strewn across the sky
Not the fluffy kind
The kind that looked like hand knitted quilts
Red, pink, orange, peach, purple
Like my favorite ice cream, sherbet
Cascading across a baby blue canvass
I pulled my phone out to take a picture of a once in a lifetime moment
You said in slow motion "yes, please, send me that"
You were driving but for a moment
It felt like the car drove itself
As we starred wide-eyed in awe watching the colors meld and melt
This morning I saw those colors again for the first time since you left
This time the moon was there too
It was as if the moon called my name
And gravity gently lifted my head to answer, "yes?"
I haven't looked up in the longest, not like before
But today it was as if the moon had something to say
So I stood there frozen in silence and listened
Wide-eyed
The moon was bright
So bright just enough for my eyes to take
The brightest I've ever seen it during daybreak
Iridescent blue
Changing from hue to hue between white, gray and blue
Fitting for what I'm going through
I miss you. I didn't think I'd ever want to see colors again
without you. But I realize those colors remind me of you

A reminder of how much I love you
Where did you go?
After you left my life snowballed into withdrawal
Colors immediately faded into a bluish gray
I preferred it that way, life in the mundane
I thought it would be too painful any other way
I've been walking around with my head down looking at the
pavement
Today I looked up and saw colors for the first time since you left
And I felt the tears swell
And I felt a smile lift my cheeks as well
I saw those same colors
I looked up and wondered if you were looking up too?
And were you looking at the same moon?
For a moment I was transported in time
We were back in the car together again
Looking up in awe
Haven't seen colors since the day you left
It was beautiful wasn't it

You feel like home

I remember the first time I saw the cosmos
It was in your deep brown eyes that held all the answers
It was in your eyes I understood how life was created
I saw a glimpse of what the heavens looked like
I find some comfort in knowing that is where you now reside

Blue Butterfly....

Are you good?

You have to remember
People can't know what they have not seen
People can't feel what they have not experienced
People will come and go because of it
But in the end what matters most
What it will ultimately all come down to is
Are you good with you?
Can you look at yourself in the mirror and say
I love you and the way you are in pain, flaws and all

My Love

You made a promise to yourself
And it seems to be a lot harder than you think it really is
Time is not on your side nor has it been the best of your friends
But time has helped you mend again and again
So time really is not all that bad
You don't like when people break promises to you
So why would you break your own promise to you
It's scary I know the thought of even trying burns you way deep
into your soul
But you don't have to be afraid anymore
You don't have to lose control
You have a good grasp of who you are
You know you have a good heart
And all you need to know
Is you are loved

I used to think modern day society lost the ability to speak our
minds clearly
Due to constructs of technology
But in reality
We subconsciously
Silenced each other
We forgot somewhere down the line
It's ok to be who you are supposed to be
Judgment comes from the egotistical mentality
It's time to shed that ego
And come into our divinity
We were all born into this world with empathy
Life just has a way to clutter our natural abilities
Until we ignore the possibilities
It's ok to be who you are supposed to be
Your soul is calling for you, crying for you
To remember you are soul beautiful

Soon

You have nothing to regret
No single soul is perfect
All we can do is try to do our best with what cards we are dealt
If I could I would take the brunt of your broken heart you think
will never get fixed
I promise you it will heal
If I could I would sword fight the demons away so that you
wouldn't have to feel this way
Stay strong my love
Remember time is the key to your questions you can't find
answers to yet
We are much stronger than we think
It will be ok...Love Sojourna

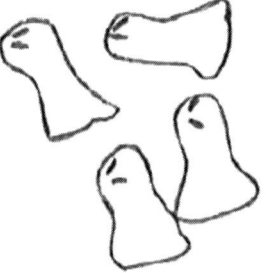

Journey

This journey will be long
It will be treacherous
It will be lonely
But it will breed song
You will climb mountains
You will cross seas
You will bear the drowning rains
You will repel the burning heat
Each step will create a new beat
Each breath creates words you soon will speak
Listen to the wind
It will create the rhythm you will soon need to move freely
Listen to mother earth
She will make it all blend and make sense
Cry if you need to
It will help you bear your aching soul
Scream if you need to
It will help you gain back control
When it's time to laugh
You will understand your journey's path
And when it's time to smile
I mean really smile for the first time in a long time
You will have reached your final mile
Your story is far from over
It is about to begin again
To be continued…

After the storm

There will be residual
Pain
Flooding inside that will need to be drained
Fallen over and broken trees that will need re-seeding
Wind damage
Wait...
There is a break in the clouds
There is a break
You will get a break
A moment to look up to the sky
A chance to breathe in the cleansed air
A moment to think
There will be a calm
No need to worry about any aftershocks
Worry is inconsequential to the bigger picture
Storms will happen, always have and always will
Storms even the most destructive to us serve a purpose
Sometimes not for us to completely understand
Storms that reoccur in our lives is to remind us
To learn something, anything from it
Rebuild
Re-group
Try something new
Or Try again
Relearn you
What did not work before it's time to let that approach go
Embrace the chance to be reborn
Take the opportunity to stop what you are currently doing
Look up and breathe again
Close your eyes
Hold your head up
Feel the air caress your skin
Dream, BIG

Be still, feel your senses flare?
That is your love telling you they are there
When you open your eyes
Believe in yourself
It's now time to walk
One foot in front of the other
The sun will come back out soon
With each step flower pedals will follow you
You will create the most beautiful colors

Imagine that in another place
Another time
We were happy
In the distance there is beauty and hope
The scenery with colors indescribable
So beautiful tears come to your eyes
These tears are not tears of pain and anguish
But tears of joy and wonderment
Seeing life from your inner child's eyes
Every sight and touch and smell are new
The sky so blue that it looked like you could swim in it
The mountains so high that you'd disappear into the sun if
standing on it
The air so soft, so warm that it feels like a lover's touch
The night sky so black that looked like you could get lost forever
Stars so bright that they shined like diamonds
Happiness and not fear
No longer afraid to live again
No longer grieving for ourselves
No longer looking for love in all the wrong places
Safe and secure
If only you could see
Please see
Please dream of love and being happy
Don't you realize they really cared?
It is possible for the pain to leave
Hand pain an eviction notice and send it packing
The moon spoke to you last night
La Luna said she'd always keep you protected
She promised you her light
It's now time for you to gracefully carry it
You took a walk alone where no one else in the world has
The only sound you could hear was the beating of your own
broken heart and god

You could hear the whisper of god speaking words to freedom
You stood upon the cliff and watched the waves crash against
the rocks
Each splash spraying cool water on your innocent face
The water became your savoir
Your clarity
As you walked into the ocean and the water rose above your
feet
Waist
Chest
Finally your face
You became free
As you reached the shore
You laid on the warm sand and smiled
You were no longer able to see the darkness
In that moment you became hope
You became love
You finally understood your place on this planet
You cried
Ready to live a life fulfilled
Don't just imagine
It can happen   133

Blue Butterfly

You want out of your cage?
You really don't know do you?
For a long time people told you that you couldn't fly with
broken wings
That it wasn't your time
You believed them, you trusted their knowledge, their
misconceived wisdom
Believed the key to the cage was held by someone else
Waiting for a reprieve from someone so you can finally breathe
A hero to come save you from your imminent soul's death
You see, your cage has always been open
Door closed for appearance
Door closed and people who told you different
Door closed but you didn't know
Fear kept you here
You can be freed
You are the hero in your story
You never on your own tried to leave
It's time to go now
Go on
Open the door,
Fly   134

Special Thank You

To my family who have always and continue to support me no matter what.

To my Grandfather Bobby whom without your help I would not have been able to share my book with the world. Thank you for always having my back, Always. You are appreciated in more ways than one. We may have a battle of the minds, but we love each other deeply. I didn't have a father growing up but I didn't need one because I had you.

To my Grandmother Silvia who is my biggest fan, you encourage me every step of the way. When my confidence in myself was lost, you found it for me and helped me believe in myself again. You're the strongest woman I know. My heart is full and I love you to the moon and back.

To my Mom Sonja who truly believes I can do no wrong, thank you for always being my cheerleader. We haven't always had it easy but I wouldn't be as kind, tough and resilient as I am without you. You were chosen to be my mom and I am thankful and I love you.

To Adrienne who has always been my kindred sister, when I was a kid I was asked in school who inspires me, my answer was you. Your work ethic and determination has always kept me grounded and motivated. I am so proud of the woman you have become you deserve every blessing you've earned. I love you.

To my friends that have listened to the laughter, the joy, the tears, the screams and the pain, and repeat. I wouldn't have come this far without you letting me be me, the good the bad the ugly and the beautiful.

To Shane Maus for graciously being a part of my first book and photographing not just me, but my sweet little old man cat Mr. Man for the author's picture. I will cherish those pictures forever. Thank you so much!

I want to say a very special thank you to Toyanna's family, her mother, father, and baby big brother. From the very beginning you accepted me into your family with open arms. I became a second daughter and sister and the love for each other has not changed. I am so grateful to you all for bringing such a beautiful, loving light, and giving soul into the world. The closeness and bond that all of you shared together, that I was lucky enough to witness firsthand was awe inspiring. I want to also thank the extended family and friends for also opening your arms to me as part of the family, you are all beautiful people. Detroit is now my second home that I love and will always hold a special place in my heart. You are an amazing family I am forever blessed to know and be a part of. I love you so much.

Thank you! I love you all!

~Sojourna

End Note

To my one and only love
Who through death, awakened my life
I miss you every second of every moment
Toy, you were my first love…
And to my cat Mr. Man my lifeline
Who has experienced it all with me
I hope one day you learn how to read ☺